# The Wounded Knee Massacre

*A Captivating Guide to the Battle of Wounded Knee and Its Impact on the Native Americans after the Final Clash between Federal Troops and the Sioux*

# Free Bonus from Captivating History (Available for a Limited time)

Hi History Lovers!

Now you have a chance to join our exclusive history list so you can get your first history ebook for free as well as discounts and a potential to get more history books for free! Simply visit the link below to join.

Captivatinghistory.com/ebook

Also, make sure to follow us on Facebook, Twitter and Youtube by searching for Captivating History.

# Contents

# Introduction

The American Indian Wars was one of the longest-running series of conflicts in modern history, as well as one of the bloodiest. During the hundreds of years of warfare between the European colonists and the local Native American tribes, countless massacres took place that was inflicted by both sides. However, by the turn of the 19$^{th}$ century, Native American tribes all over the continent had grown significantly weaker, both in numbers and in their inability to keep pace with the innovations of Western weaponry. Most of the civilian population of the major Native American tribes were moved onto reservations as the US government pushed for more and more territory, expanding into the heart of the continent.

While initially the borders of the reservations were acceptable for many of the Native American tribes, the government started reneging on the old treaties after the 1840s and started stealing prime reservation land, completely displacing many of the Native American tribes from their ancestral grounds. Naturally, many of the Native Americans weren't too happy about this, leading to the last of the major conflicts in the American Indian Wars, including the Ute Wars and the Apache Wars that extended from the second half of the 19$^{th}$ century to the first quarter of the 20$^{th}$ century. This is one of the darkest periods of American history, considering the fact that during this period, the US government manipulated the public sentiment against the Native Americans, allowing the US military to carry out many atrocities against the Native Americans, the most notable of which being the Wounded Knee Massacre of 1890.

Unlike Custer's Last Stand (the Battle of the Little Bighorn), which was an act of war, the Wounded Knee Massacre was out and out genocide against unarmed civilians. This event finally raised concerns regarding how the Native Americans were being exploited and oppressed by the government, but it would still take another three and a half decades before any significant measures were taken by the government to officially put an end to the American Indian Wars. Naturally, due to its sensitive nature in American history, the Wounded Knee Massacre is often glossed over in textbooks, talking about the event in a generalized manner. But such a generalized representation undermines the real impact and significance of the events that happened on that fateful day, making it one of the most tragic events in Native American history.

In 1973, on the same spot of the Wounded Knee Massacre, a 71-day siege took place in response to the racial injustice faced by the Native Americans on the reservation from the local white population of Minneapolis. The response against this discrimination was headed by Dennis Banks and Leonard Peltier of AIM (American Indian Movement) and initially started as a protest but later turned into a full-fledged siege that attracted the spotlight of the mainstream media regarding the terrible conditions of Native Americans living on reservations.

To establish the facts of what occurred, most of the details taken into account in this book while analyzing and discussing the events of the Wounded Knee Massacre are taken from the records of the American participants of the war, as well as from military records of the investigation into what happened and the subsequent trial of one of the participants of the massacre. In this book, we aim to provide the reader with a more in-depth look at the factors and major players that played a role in the Wounded Knee Massacre, as well as the significance of its aftermath.

# Chapter 1- A Short Introduction of the Lakota Tribe and the Ghost Dance Movement

The Lakota were the primary victims of the Wounded Knee Massacre, not the Sioux, as many mistakenly assume. The Sioux were a coalition of tribes that lived in the northern Great Plains, with the Lakota being one of them. The Lakota, in turn, were divided into seven sub-tribes, with the Hunkpapa being the most famous since the prominent figure Sitting Bull, who led the Great Sioux War of 1876, was its leader at one point in history. While the Battle of the Little Bighorn, which was one of the opening conflicts of the war, was an immediate victory for the Native Americans, the long-term political and social impacts afterward were detrimental for them. Many other tribes suffered as well, as the government and the press twisted Custer's legacy in such a way that the public demanded stricter measures against the Native Americans, allowing the government to use the US military force, as well as the Native American reservations, to suppress and oppress the Native American population.

It should be noted that the Lakota are not limited to only the United States —today, a significant number live in Canada as well, though they are not considered as "treaty Indians" over there (a treaty Indian is someone who belongs to a band that is a party to one of the eleven Numbered Treaties, which were signed by Canada and various First Nations tribes). The American settlers first came into contact with the Lakota during the Lewis and Clark Expedition in 1804, and although the two groups did not get along, there were no outright hostilities between the two. Things seemed to take a turn for the better between the Lakota and the US military when the Lakota allied themselves with the US Army in 1823 in their efforts against the Arikara in the Arikara War. However, this union was short-lived as the construction of Fort Laramie, which would go on to become the prime fur trading outpost in the Great Plains for years to come, was constructed on Lakota land without their permission, complicating relationships with the settlers. Frequent Native American raids and attacks on the settlers living in and around the settlement were common until 1851when the Treaty of Fort Laramie was signed, making it safe for settlers to travel along the Oregon Trail for a few years before relationships deteriorated once again, permanently this time.

While the US government acknowledged the sovereignty of the Lakota tribe in the Black Hills region, in practice, they did nothing to stop the influx of settlers who settled in Lakota lands instead of just passing through as the treaty had ordained. As a result, the Lakota resumed their attacks on the settlers, which prompted an attack on a Lakota village in Nebraska in 1855. The attack was led by General William Harney, and it was labeled as a counterattack on the Lakota due to the Grattan massacre, which sparked the First Sioux War. Despite the Grattan massacre being instigated by Lieutenant John Grattan and a mixed-race interpreter named Lucian Auguste as testified by a local outpost trader named James Bordeaux, whom the Lakota called to help interpret with the military as the conversation between Conquering Bear, a Brulé Lakota chief, and Lieutenant Grattan grew more heated. By the time Bordeaux arrived, things were already out of hand, with the Lakota warriors of the village readying themselves to attack the American soldiers. Grattan ended the discussion and headed back to his men, but a stray shot from a random soldier managed to hit a Lakota warrior. All 31 men accompanying Gratton were killed, with one dying from his wounds later; however, they managed to wound Conquering Bear as well, and he died later from his wounds.

After the First Sioux War (1854 to 1856) and the Dakota War (1862), the conflicts stopped temporarily due to the American Civil War, but they resumed once again after the war had ended and settlers once again began to encroach Native American lands. When mining operations started in the Great Plains in 1866, the US government directly breached the Treaty of Fort Laramie by establishing military outposts along the Bozeman Trail to safeguard the settlers and prospectors traveling along the route. After two years of hard fighting, a new Treaty of Fort Laramie was signed, once again, with promises of the US government to not encroach the Black Hills region in the future. But the government reneged on the treaty yet again when gold was discovered in 1872 in the Black Hills region. This time, the government dropped all pretenses and started an open campaign to suppress and subjugate the Sioux tribes once and for all in order to have total control of the Great Basin region.

The Battle of the Little Bighorn made it easier for the US government and military to sway public opinion to allow them to carry out their actions unhindered. This also led to the indiscriminate killing of bison in the Great Plains region, which destroyed the Native American economy and their way of life. Bison were crucial to the tribal lifestyle for two primary reasons, food and hide, the latter being a large part in trade and commerce. General Philip Sheridan correctly deduced that by deliberately destroying their primary food source, it would be easier to force them onto Native American reservations, making them dependent on government-issued supplies in order to survive. As such, he encouraged his soldiers, as well as new settlers, to hunt down as many bison as possible, even if they didn't need the meat, which almost drove the bison population to extinction by the end of the 19th century. After the Great Sioux War ended in 1877, most of the Lakota resigned themselves to their grim fates and moved to reservations, as their numbers had dwindled greatly due to the constant warfare for almost half a century. Even the mighty Sitting Bull had to flee to Canada to escape the US Army's grasp but eventually returned and surrendered due to the lack of food and supplies in 1881.

The overall situation made many of the tribes on the reservations despondent, and they found solace in a new religion called the Ghost Dance beginning in 1889. The basic premise of the Ghost Dance religion is very interesting, as it combines aspects of Christianity.

The religion was reignited by a Paiute medicine man named Wovoka, also christened Jack Wilson. We say reignited because there is a popular misconception that Wovoka founded the Ghost Dance religion; that is not the case. The Ghost Dance movement first made its appearance among the Northern Paiutes in the 1870s, and Wovoka's father was one of the few who took up the religion at that time and taught the customs to his son. According to Wovoka, he received a vision from the Christian God, who took him to heaven and showed him the spirits of past Native Americans who were happily residing there. He also claimed that God revealed that Jesus Christ would be Native American and appear among them in 1892, and when that happened, everyone would be elevated to a state of eternal bliss. But to achieve this golden age, the Native Americans would have to abhor all types of violence and engage themselves in religious prayers. The prayer took form in the ancient Native American custom of a spirit dance, which was misleadingly translated as "Ghost Dance" by interpreters, giving it an ominous feel to those unfamiliar with Native American customs.

Wovoka claimed to be a prophet, and as a result, most of the Native American tribes sent emissaries to verify his claims. Wovoka's charisma won over many of these emissaries, who became fervent converts, spreading the word of the Ghost Dance religion to their respective tribes upon returning home. This allowed it to rapidly turn popular in a very short period of time, which unnerved both the US government and the military, who both grew apprehensive of the new religion and its influence. But to be accurate, it wasn't the concept of the Ghost Dance ritual that unnerved them. Initially, when it was conceived, the Ghost Dance ritual only involved adorning oneself in paint before taking part in the dance, which was actually a shuffle done in silence to a slow, single drumbeat. But later on, another element was added to it known as Ghost shirts. According to the Ghost Dance shamans, wearing these shirts that were inscribed with ritualistic pictography would protect the wearer from the white man's bullets. The US military feared that such an element that promised invulnerability might promote aggressive behavior from the Ghost Dancers.

Initially, the Lakota were not very interested in the new religion, as their living conditions were worsening day by day. To top it off, in early 1890, the territory for the Lakota reservation was further reduced, which led to the government attempting to turn the Lakota into an agricultural-based society. They were provided with the training and farming equipment, but ultimately, the effort failed, mainly due to the poor soil conditions of the reduced reservation land. The US government, however, would not take that as an excuse, and to encourage productivity, the government rations for the Lakota were cut in half that year. In their despair, the Lakota turned to the new Ghost Dance religion to distract themselves from their misfortune. Sadly, one such Ghost Dance ceremony went very awry, leading to the Wounded Knee Massacre.

# Chapter 2- A Brief Overview of the Relationship between the US Government and the Native American Population of America

We would like to begin this chapter with a little story. On January 7th, 1891, a Brulé Lakota named Plenty Horses shot and killed US Lieutenant Edward W. Casey. After committing this act, Plenty Horses calmly waited for members of the local law enforcement to take him to jail. When he was asked why he did what he had done in court, he gave the following answer:

> Five years I attended Carlisle and was educated in the ways of the white man. When I returned to my people, I was an outcast among them. I was no longer an Indian. I was not a white man. I was lonely. I shot the lieutenant so I might make a place for myself among my people. I am now one of them. I shall be hung, and the Indians will bury me as a warrior.

Plenty Horse was one of the few progressive Lakota who decided to embrace the Western culture and the city lifestyle. To achieve his goal, he left his tribe on the Pine Ridge Reservation, also known as the Pine Ridge Agency, in 1885 to pursue an education in Carlisle, Pennsylvania. Tragically, the day he came back to his home after finishing his education, he had to bury his loved ones. His decision to be educated in the Western ways had isolated him from his people, and stricken by grief, he murdered Lieutenant Casey eight days after his family was killed in the Wounded Knee Massacre. Hearing his story, the visibly shaken judge immediately dismissed all the charges against him and allowed him to go as a free man.

What was the reason for this sudden erratic decision? One might tend to think that the judge had a soft heart, but that was not the case. What really happened was that Plenty Horses' lawyers had found a loophole. The lawyers argued that a state of war existed in the Pine Ridge region at the time of the murder, and as a rule of war, if two parties involved in a conflict kill one another, then a death sentence was null since the death of the other party would be considered as an act of war. The lawyers also further argued that if Plenty Horses was charged with murder and given a death sentence, then it should be applicable for all the US soldiers who participated at the Wounded Knee Massacre. This logic was so infallible that the US Army sent in an officer to testify that a state of war did indeed exist on the Pine Ridge Reservation at that time to avoid murder charges for the entire military unit that had been involved. Thus, Plenty Horses walked free, with all charges dismissed. The point of this story is to exemplify how far the US government and military infrastructure were willing to go to cover up the Wounded Knee Massacre from the public eye.

As the age-old saying goes, it takes two to tango. That is indeed the case for almost all major conflicts across the world since the dawn of time. A conflict can be called a battle only when both sides are capable of putting up a fight. But when one side loses that ability, and the other side continuously pushes for the conflict to keep going, it no longer remains a battle; it becomes genocide. The reason for such a somber introduction is to ease American readers into the idea that certain versions of American history that they had learned from history books and museums are far from the truth, and one should not be uncomfortable with learning the hard facts. Since this book tends to lean on the conclusion that the Wounded Knee Massacre was a perpetuated plan by a hateful and racist US regime, some readers might take offense, citing the many accounts and books that clearly indicate that either the event was an accident or that the Lakota attacked first. We would like to also add that this is a history book detailing facts and does not serve as the platform for any agenda, and the discussions and analyses made in this book are logical and cross-reference different accounts of the event. So, it's up to the reader to decide whether they want to accept reality or the propaganda that they have grown up with, which can be a bit difficult due to the fact that most history books, as well the US military archives, still list this massacre as a "battle."

Many historians often accept many atrocities as a necessary evil to the advancement of civilization, and up to a certain extent, that sentiment is understandable. Let's say if the Indian subcontinent, as well as the African and American continents, were never colonized and had been left in relative peace by European pioneers, would the world look like the way it does today? Slavery, racism, and oppression are definitely the byproducts of colonialism, but it also cannot be denied that most parts of the world are technologically and culturally uniform thanks to colonization. It has allowed the Western culture to serve as a relatable and common basis for people of all races around the world, allowing us to communicate more effectively. But as a result, the significance and impact of many atrocities and genocides committed by Western settlers and colonists all across the globe until the beginning of the $21^{st}$ century are often toned down in the general curriculum and in general history books. This is also the case of the history of the last 75 years of the American Indian Wars until it formally ended in 1924.

However, it's not like the relationships between the settlers and the Native Americans were very friendly to begin with. While the relationship between the European settlers and the Native American tribes were fairly cordial in the beginning when America was an uncharted and unexplored "New World," by the mid-half of the 19<sup>th</sup> century, the Americans and the Native Americans almost always had daggers drawn on each other. As the former European colonies centralized under one unified government, they no longer were at war with themselves. To sustain the economy and to develop it, the only choice for the new nation was to expand as rapidly as possible by acquiring more land and resources for industrialization. And all the prime land was inhabited by the Native Americans, who were very unwilling to let go of their means of life as well as their culture and traditions. When the US government realized that they could not convince the Native Americans to just sell their land, they opted for a policy that saw the systematic elimination of the Native American population all across the North American continent.

In the Great Plains, the damage was very serious. Mining opportunities, especially gold, drove people from all walks of life to travel along the Oregon Trail. As a result, the region saw a series of bloody conflicts and massacres. Most of the conflicts started because the US government refused to acknowledge many of the peace treaties made with the Native Americans in the earlier part of the 19<sup>th</sup> century. The general pattern of the American Indian Wars during this period was similar to the following: the Native American tribes would refuse to let settlers encroach their land and started fighting back, the local government officials would call it an emergency, and then the US military would start a fight with the local tribe or tribes to suppress and relocate them to government reservations. Most of the time, fighting was not even involved— there are many listed instances where the US military slaughtered unarmed civilians and termed the event as a "battle," which just happens to be the case with the Wounded Knee Massacre. There are over eighty listed massacres from both sides during this period, as the Native Americans were not entirely innocent and perpetrated some horrible crimes themselves. But it should be noted that the Native Americans were often forced to do so due to the constant encroachment of their lands and livelihood. Some of the major massacres on the Native Americans during the later 19<sup>th</sup> century include the Bridge Gulch massacre, the Yontoket massacre, the Achulet massacre, and the Grande Ronde River Valley massacre. In almost all of these cases, the victims were unarmed civilians and children. And while the US government did grant Native Americans full US citizenship in 1924, they faced as much racism and bigotry as African Americans by the general public and law enforcement agencies.

Taking all of this information into context, we can easily agree upon the fact that the relationship between the Native Americans and the European Americans were never that great, as the chain of greed and unbroken promises continuously hampered the growth of their relationship. The Wounded Knee Massacre was no different—in fact, the funny thing is that despite their constant claims of Indian savagery and barbarity, when one tallies the American and Native American death tolls from the 19<sup>th</sup> century, the number of Native American civilian casualties is tenfold of that of American casualties. But historians turned a blind eye on these facts for a long time, which has resulted in the distorted public image that the Wounded Knee Massacre has taken. This continues even to the present day, as many believe that it was a tragic accident.

# Chapter 3- A Brief Overview of the Key Players of the Wounded Knee Massacre

In this chapter of the book, we will be taking a glimpse at the lives of the key historical figures of the Wounded Knee Massacre to gain some insight into their actions on that fateful day.

## Major General Nelson A. Miles

By the end of the 19th century, it was highly unusual for the American settlers to sympathize with the plight of the Native Americans. Only European newspapers seemed to see the situation for what it was—a gradual mass genocide. Despite the unhealthy political and public opinion regarding the Native Americans at that time, Nelson A. Miles turned out to be one of the first, and most vocal, Native American rights activists. His attitude and conduct in regard to the anti-Indian government policies eventually made him so unpopular that there was a general sense of relief when he retired.

Unlike many of the high-ranking officials in the US military, Nelson Appleton Miles came from humble origins. Born to a simple farming family on August 8th, 1839, in Westminster, Massachusetts, Miles had a relatively simple childhood. He attended the local school until he became a teenager, at which point he moved to Boston. He was also exceptional in the fact that he didn't attend West Point, as many of his peers had done. After moving to Boston, Miles had the opportunity to read a lot of books on military history and tactics, which he read late at night after his day's work was done. For practical drills and lessons, he turned to a retired French officer in Boston who took a liking to him and tutored him. When the Civil War broke out, Miles finally joined the military. As a part of the 22nd Massachusetts Volunteer Infantry, he was commissioned as a lieutenant in 1861. He took part in his first battle in the Battle of Seven Pines the following year under the command of Brigadier General Oliver Howard. Miles was wounded in battle, but he had displayed admirable bravery in his first skirmish, so after his recuperation, he was promoted to lieutenant colonel.

After being transferred to the 61$^{st}$ New York Infantry Division, Miles would eventually go on to participate in the Battle of Antietam, where he received a full promotion to colonel for displaying further bravery. He led two more battles during the Civil War, the Battle of Fredericksburg and the Battle of Chancellorsville. During the Battle of Chancellorsville, Miles was gravely wounded, having been shot in the neck and abdomen. Miles was awarded a Medal of Honor for his performance in that battle but ended up missing the pivotal Battle of Gettysburg due to his wounds. Once he recovered, he would go on to become one of the most accomplished commanders in the Civil War, leading the US Army against the Confederates in the Battles of the Wilderness and Spotsylvania Court House under the command of Major General Scott Hancock. He was later transferred to General Ulysses Grant's (who would go on to become the president of the United States) regiment, where he took part in Grant's Overland Campaign. By the time the Civil War had ended, Miles had achieved a meteoric rise in the US military ranks, achieving the rank of major general of volunteers by only the age of 26.

Despite this success, the post-Civil War time period was not kind to him due to his own overambitious nature. His achievement as a soldier won him the rank of colonel in the US Army after the war, a far higher post than many of the West Point graduates who had similar performances in the Civil War. But for Miles, who was eyeing for the position of general, this wasn't enough. So, he chose the western frontier as the next place to prove himself. Taking command of the 5th Infantry Regiment in 1869, he would take part in multiple military campaigns in the Great Plains for the next two decades. In fact, after Custer's defeat in the Battle of the Little Bighorn, Miles was the one who cracked down on the Lakota and Dakota tribes in the Great Plains over the winter of 1876. Miles oversaw the operations from Fort Keogh and made most of the Lakota and Northern Cheyenne surrender and move to the Great Sioux Reservation. His other notable achievement during this period was the establishment of heliograph lines as a primary means of safe communication for the US military in the Great Plains.

After two decades of frontier life, Miles was finally promoted to major general in 1890, the same year that the Wounded Knee Massacre happened. After the American Indian Wars unofficially ended with the Wounded Knee Massacre (the conflicts would still continue, but they were much smaller in size than before), Miles would spend the last active years of his military career planning and coordinating the Spanish-American War, from which he was politically sidelined from participating. In 1903, General Miles finally retired from the military and spent the rest of his days in relative unpopularity and obscurity. This was because after retiring from the US Army, Miles dedicated his time to be one of the first vocal Native American rights activists. His activism led to the 1917 and 1920 investigations into the events of the Wounded Knee Massacre. Nelson died in 1925 from a heart attack while attending a circus with his grandchildren.

Despite being unpopular during his life due to his clashes with President Benjamin Harrison and the top military brass in the years following the Wounded Knee Massacre, Miles is probably the only US Army officer today who is respectfully remembered thanks to his attempts to right the wrongs of the American government and its people. Though Miles did not live to see his legacy fulfilled, he definitely played a key role in starting the spark that started the fire for Native American rights activism in America.

## James W. Forsyth

A relatively low-key figure in the military before the Wounded Knee Massacre, Forsyth was known to be a dependable officer, even if he was not one of the best. Born into a family of average income, Forsyth attended local schools before enrolling in West Point Academy in 1851. He studied and graduated from West Point in 1856 with the sole intent of joining the army. After graduation, he was stationed to the 9th US Infantry and commissioned as the second lieutenant.

After spending a few years in idyllic postings at San Juan island and the Washington Territory, Forsyth eventually joined the Union side in the American Civil War. When he joined the 64th Ohio Infantry, he was promoted to the rank of colonel. Despite his high ranking, Forsyth was not a very proficient soldier. During his tenure in the US Army during the American Civil War, he served as inspector general, aide-de-camp, provost marshal, and chief of staff to the Army of Potomac, the Army of Shenandoah, and General Grant's forces in his Overland Campaign. Throughout the war, Forsyth was a vocal supporter of the Buffalo Soldiers, the new African American unit that was formed to fight the Confederates. In light of his early military service, one could call Forsyth a man of political nature as all of his roles constituted the maintenance of communication and discipline within the rank-and-file soldiers.

Despite his passive role in the Civil War, Forsyth actively participated in military campaigns in the American Indian Wars after being appointed secretary, and then later inspector, of the Department of Missouri in 1866. As a US Army officer, he also had the privilege of going to Europe to act as an observer in the Franco-Prussian War in 1870. After his return from Europe, Forsyth participated in the Bannock War of 1878 and eventually went on to formulate the curriculum for artillery training for the US Army. In 1886, Forsyth was promoted to colonel and assumed the command of the 7th US Cavalry. He then marched to Fort Riley, Kansas, where he remained in his post until November 1890.

Besides playing a key role in the events of the Wounded Knee Massacre, Forsyth also fought in the Drexel Mission Fight the following day before being relieved of command by Miles himself. After the massacre, he was put on trial as per Major General Miles' request for an inquiry into his conduct. After the completion of the inquiry, though, he was praised for his bravery in the "Battle" of Wounded Knee. Following these events, he was also promoted to the rank of brigadier general in 1894 before eventually being promoted to major general in 1897. Forsyth passed away in Ohio in 1906 after a lifetime of military service.

**Spotted Elk**

Spotted Elk is the English translation for the Native American name *Uŋpȟáŋ Glešká*, which is also spelled as *Hupah Gleška*. The exact date of his birth is not confirmed, but it is estimated to have been between 1820 to 1826. As the son of Miniconjou Chief Lone Horse, Spotted Elk succeeded his father in 1877.[1]

---

[1] The Miniconjou are a subdivision of the Lakota.

Both before and after his ascension as the leader of his tribe, he was known to be a man of peace and a very skilled diplomat. But that didn't mean Spotted Elk was lacking courage; he participated in the Great Sioux War with his half-brother Sitting Bull and his nephew Crazy Horse, along with other Sioux chiefs. But as we know from history, their victory at the Battle of the Little Bighorn ended up blowing back on the Sioux, who were doggedly pursued and suppressed by the US Army, forcing them to either flee to Canada with Sitting Bull or to retreat to the government-allotted reservation lands.

Spotted Elk was one of the first Sioux leaders to give in to the government's demands, and he tried to ensure that his people embraced the "white man's way" to guarantee their survival. In the 1880s, he tried his best to curry government favor in Washington to improve the condition of his tribe by expanding their education, but it ultimately fell on deaf ears. After years of vain attempts, Spotted Elk finally relegated himself to the confines of his village until the events that led to the death of Sitting Bull. After Sitting Bull died, members of his tribes traveled to take refuge with Spotted Elk, who led his band to the Pine Ridge Reservation after Chief Red Cloud invited him. However, before they could make it there, the US Army caught up with them, leading to the events of the massacre. This beloved Miniconjou chief breathed his last at the Wounded Knee Massacre, along with up to 300 other victims.

# Chapter 4- Prelude to the Wounded Knee Massacre

While it may be easy to blame the US Army as the villains for letting things get out of hand, the truth is somewhat more complicated. The fault lay with the Indian agency responsible for overseeing the Lakota reservation at that time. The Wounded Knee Massacre is one of the many scenarios in which the government-appointed Indian agencies failed to carry out their basic responsibility of interacting and communicating with the Native Americans on the reservation, which was what the position was originally intended for. Many of the reservation agents appointed in the latter half of the 19<sup>th</sup> century were racists, bigots, and religious fanatics who tried to degrade and Westernize the Native Americans residing in the agencies against their will. Two such individuals were Daniel F. Royer of the Pine Ridge Indian Agency and James McLaughlin of the Standing Rock Agency. Both men were extremely paranoid and irrational, with Royer requesting military intervention against the Ghost Dancers as soon as he was appointed to the position since he didn't like the new religion. To this end, he made false claims of violence and uprisings, which led the US Army to send a detachment of soldiers to verify and control the situation after President Benjamin Harrison felt pressured by the "Indian menace," as the newspapers called it. The main objective of the military mobilization was to capture Sitting Bull and a few other chiefs to put an end to what the American authorities termed the "Messiah Craze."

To have a deeper understanding of what went down during the Wounded Knee Massacre, one has to understand the importance and significance of the second Treaty of Fort Laramie that was signed in 1868. The main outline of the treaty is as follows:

- The US government would provide reparations for damages caused to the Native Americans in the recent Red Cloud's War, as well as for past conflicts.

- Any criminal dispute involving a white settler would be resolved through the government agent appointed for the Native American reservation.

- Decisions regarding reservation land would be totally up to the Sioux with no interference from the US government.

- If the US government wanted to cede reservation territory in the future, they would have to undertake a vote for the proposed resolution and receive three-fourths of the votes of grown Native American men in favor of the resolution who resided on the reservation.

As mentioned before, the US government broke most of the conditions of the treaty. While this caused resentment among the inhabitants of the reservation, since their overall lifestyle was not affected, they mostly accepted these violations in a disgruntled manner. But the US government crossed the line in 1877 when it tried to occupy the Black Hills region. This finally exhausted the patience of the Sioux as the Black Hills territory was their chief hunting ground as it was full of game. Thanks to this part of the reservation, they didn't really have to depend on government supplies to survive. But all this changed when gold was found in the region, and on February 28th, the US Congress bypassed the Treaty of Fort Laramie with the Agreement of 1877. The summary of this act boiled down to the US government declaring that they intended to purchase the Black Hill region from the Native Americans. As it encompassed 7.3 million acres of land, the ownership of the Black Hills land was tantamount to the survival of the Native Americans if they didn't want to rely on the government for assistance. The American settlers and soldiers had already wiped out most of the bison population from the Great Plains, making the Black Hills the last remaining hunting and fishing ground for the Great Plains tribes. The reservation borders were forcefully redrawn, and while the Black Hills Act mentioned that the land had been purchased from the Sioux, no transactions were actually made, a fact that was acknowledged 103 years later by the US justice system in 1980.

Over the next decade, the bison population in the Great Plains was nearly driven to extinction. In 1888, things started to get dicey again when the government beef supplies for the Great Sioux Reservation were spoiled by anthrax under mysterious circumstances, signaling that hard years of starvation would soon follow. In 1889, the General Allotment Act, also known as the Dawes Act, was forcefully enacted by the US government, which divided the single Great Sioux Reservation into five smaller ones—Standing Rock, Cheyenne River, Rosebud, Pine Ridge, and Lower Brule. After being placed under public pressure to deal with the "Ghost Dance menace," as the newspapers termed it, President Benjamin Harrison allowed the military to take control of the situation. The military forces dispatched by Washington were led by General Nelson A. Miles, who was a pragmatic man who hoped to resolve the racial tensions peacefully. While on his way to the Pine Ridge Agency, he sent the following telegram to John Schofield, the commanding general of the US Army, on December 19th, four days after Sitting Bull had died.

> The difficult Indian problem cannot be solved permanently at this end of the line. It requires the fulfillment of Congress of the treaty obligations that the Indians were entreated and

coerced into signing. They signed away a valuable portion of their reservation, and it is now occupied by white people, for which they have received nothing.

They understood that ample provision would be made for their support; instead, their supplies have been reduced, and much of the time they have been living on half and two-thirds rations. Their crops, as well as the crops of the white people, for two years have been almost total failures.

The dissatisfaction is wide spread, especially among the Sioux, while the Cheyennes have been on the verge of starvation, and were forced to commit depredations to sustain life. These facts are beyond question, and the evidence is positive and sustained by thousands of witnesses.

Unfortunately, this letter did not make it to the public eye until long after the events of Wounded Knee had passed. American newspapers (other than the local ones) were too busy portraying the tense situation at Pine Ridge, and it is highly doubtful whether the letter would ultimately have had any impact on changing public opinion at that time anyway.

It has to be mentioned that the newspapers at that time were just as much at fault for straining reality and planting the seeds of falsehood as the reservation agents involved in the incident were. In the aftermath of the events of the Battle of the Little Bighorn, national publications showed its power by twisting public opinion to great effect, which allowed the government and military to quell the Great Sioux War with brute force. In the case of the Wounded Knee Massacre, the press had been adding fuel to the fire beforehand by manufacturing fancy stories of intrigue and "Indian savagery" that pushed the public to demand the government to intervene before it led to another Native American uprising. Even after the massacre happened, most newspapers continued supporting the government. William Fitch Kelley, a Nebraskan reporter who was the only active correspondent on the scene with the military on that fateful day, played a huge role in muddling the events of the massacre by later reporting that it was the Native Americans who opened fire first, a statement that was contradicted by George Bartlett, a lawman-cum-storekeeper stationed near Wounded Knee. Incidentally, he was also a legendary gunslinger and had a reputation as an honorable man. His testimony also bears importance as he was one of the few individuals sent by the US government to coax the Native Americans into being more peaceful since he had friendly relations with them and spoke their language. His post as a US marshal, though, was suddenly taken from him after the Wounded Knee Massacre. His statements were first recorded after he started working as a traveling showman in the late 1890s.

The primary directive for the initial expedition was to apprehend Sitting Bull, who was still the most influential figure in the Lakota community due to his victories in the Great Sioux War. When the government decided to cut down the rations for his tribe, Sitting Bull had no choice but to let the people of his tribe embrace the new Ghost Dance religion, as opposing it would have compromised the integrity of his leadership. Though most of his loyal followers practiced the new religion, multiple sources indicate that Sitting Bull himself didn't take up the new faith. It's not clear what drove James McLaughlin to override military orders and take actions beyond his jurisdiction, but what is known is that just before the military arrived, he sent around 35 to 40 reservation police officers to arrest Sitting Bull and bring him into custody. Sitting Bull refused to go with the officers, and a fight broke out when the police tried to forcefully arrest Sitting Bull. One of Sitting Bull's followers named Catch-the-Bear fired the first shot, injuring Lieutenant Bullhead, who, surprisingly, decided to shoot Sitting Bull in the chest with his revolver instead of his actual attacker. A police officer named Red Tomahawk then shot Sitting Bull in the head, who then dropped to the ground and later died from his wounds.

Many historians take this as damning evidence that the whole affair was a set-up to get an excuse to kill the old Lakota chief who held so much influence in the Native American communities to spark a conflict. Further eyewitness accounts from multiple sources, including one George Bartlett, has helped to confirm this theory over the years. But what happened instead of an uprising was that many of the Lakota escaped the reservation outright throughout the following days. Around 200 Lakota escaped to the Cheyenne River Reservation to join Spotted Elk, but within a short while, Spotted Elk headed to the Pine Ridge Agency after Chief Red Cloud, a leader of the Oglala Lakota, invited him. Spotted Elk was followed by Sitting Bull's former followers as well as 150 Hunkpapa tribesmen, consisting of only 38 warriors. Although he was initially thinking of just staying at his village, Spotted Elk feared that doing so would only result in another scenario like Sitting Bull's incident, so he headed toward Pine Ridge after receiving an invitation from Chief Red Cloud. According to recorded Indian oral history, Spotted Elk had been initially reluctant about leaving the village and did his best to convince the others to stay, but many of Sitting Bull's followers grew uncomfortable and urged him to leave. After some debate, Spotted Elk and his followers fled from their reservation to head south on December 23rd, 1890. The weather was extremely hostile, as they were traveling in the middle of winter, and Spotted Elk caught pneumonia within two days of the journey.

The military finally caught up with the belligerent Lakota on December 28th, forcing them to a halt. They escorted the Native Americans to nearby Wounded Knee Creek, which was about five miles to the west. By this time, Spotted Elk's health had dropped significantly, and he was almost on his deathbed when he was called out by the commander of the US forces to meet outside his tent. An extremely sick Spotted Elk was carried outside to meet Colonel James Forsyth, who had arrived the previous evening with the rest of the 7th Calvary, on the afternoon of December 29th, 1890. Earlier in the morning, the colonel had ordered a search for weapons among the Native American tents, which yielded 38 rifles in total, although more were discovered as they continued to search. The majority of these rifles were hunting weapons and had a comparatively antiquated design compared to the US Army weaponry at the time, which also included the Hotchkiss-designed M1875 mountain guns (mini-cannons which fired artillery shells), of which four were set up around the encampment. Apparently, Colonel Forsyth was not satisfied with the number of weapons they had found and demanded that Spotted Elk tell his tribesmen to give up any hidden weapons. It is at this point that the American and Native American version of the events that followed diverge from one another substantially.

# Chapter 5- The Wounded Knee Massacre and the Truth behind the Events

The actual events of the massacre took place within a very short period of time. But it is these actions that raise a lot of questions. Before taking a gander at those questions, let's have a look at events of the Wounded Knee Massacre.

Although the two versions of the narrative diverge, both versions agree on some key points. As mentioned in the previous chapter, the Lakota under Spotted Elk's banner started their expedition toward the Pine Ridge Reservation on December 23rd, 1890. Spotted Elk and his train were twenty miles northeast of the Pine Ridge Agency when the Lakota were stopped and forced to camp at Wounded Knee Creek for the night. Colonel Forsyth arrived later that evening, bringing the total number of US soldiers to 500. In sharp contrast, the Lakota only numbered 350, with 230 of them being men and 120 being women and children. The following morning, Forsyth began his conversations with the Lakota, agitating an increasingly tense situation.

In the midst of the heated exchange of words, a medicine man named Yellow Bird began the Ghost Dance, which is performed in a slow, rhythmic fashion, alarming the soldiers who saw the dance as the prelude to warfare. This reportedly brought an aggressive reaction out of the Native American warriors around Yellow Bird, who started chanting with him and shouting at the American soldiers. These actions prompted Forsyth to conduct a second weapons search (which is confirmed by military records to be true) when Spotted Elk was carried out on a stretcher to converse with Forsyth. While the two were conversing, the US soldiers were conducting the search. During it, they came across a Lakota man named Black Coyote, who refused to give up his weapon. Black Coyote was deaf and did not understand much English, and since he adamantly refused to give up his gun, it led to a scuffle with the soldiers. A shot was fired during the scuffle, after which both sides started firing on each other. Everything was over in a matter of minutes, and when the smoke finally cleared, between 250 and 300 Lakota were lying dead in the camp, including Spotted Elk. Fifty-one of the Lakota were wounded, with seven of them dying later from their wounds, meaning that every Lakota that was present at the camp either died or were injured from the devasting attack. The US Army had 64 casualties, with 39 of them being injuries, although some did die later from their wounds. Incidentally, most of the casualties on the American side were caused by their own Hotchkiss guns.

Though the massacre was over, the conflict was not completely suppressed that day. The following day, another fight took place on the Pine Ridge Reservation known as the Drexel Mission Fight, which again saw Forsyth dealing with the Lakota. The Native Americans on the reservation had supposedly burned down the Catholic Mission, and Forsyth, his eight troops, and a battery of artillery became engaged with the Brulé Lakota from the Rosebud Reservation as they tried to determine if there was any truth to the story. The fierce attack almost brought the 7th Cavalry to certain defeat, but they were rescued by a Buffalo Soldier regiment of the 9th

Cavalry led by Major Guy V. Henry. This event was ignored by most newspapers at the time, but it was a key point in the investigation trial started by General Miles.

From the many versions of the events of the Wounded Knee Massacre, these are the commonly established facts. The archeological proof is sadly moot due to the fact that the dead Lakota were buried unceremoniously in an unmarked mass grave. If one takes a look at the various historical publications on the Wounded Knee Massacre from the many different authors on the internet, one will come across at least seven to eight different versions of the events. So, what we will try to do is take the most accepted and credible versions of the massacre from the US Army and Lakota and analyze them to root out the discrepancies and form a clear and concise picture of the events that followed.

Forsyth was not fluent in the Lakota tongue, and so, he took a half-blood Sioux translator named Philip Wells along with him. Wells was the only person in the entire detachment who could understand and speak the Lakota language, which raises suspicions as to whether Wells alone was responsible for the misunderstanding between the US Army and the already on-edge Lakota. His half-breed heritage might have been motivation enough—Native Americans were usually highly disdainful of mixed heritage even when it came to their own tribes, so it stands to reason that Wells would have had a rough time growing up among the Native Americans, leading him to make things difficult for them. Then there is also the fact that his version of events varies wildly from the testimony of many of the soldiers participating in the events of Wounded Knee.

According to Wells, the Lakota were starting to talk suspiciously after the first search was conducted and the small caliber hunting rifles had been retrieved. All the families were lined outside their tepees while the soldiers rummaged through their belongings, looking for weapons. It was also at this point that the women and children were separated from the men, an important point to keep in mind as we discuss and analyze the credibility of the US version of the events. This apparently prompted him to report to Major Samuel Whitside that the Lakota men were up to some mischief, causing Colonel Forsyth to order the second search.

Up to this point, Wells' statement doesn't greatly vary from the other accounts of the massacre. The contradiction starts when he stated that as soon as Yellow Bird finished his dance and sat down, some of the Lakota men who were standing on the sidelines to watch the meeting between Spotted Elk and Colonel Forsyth started firing at the US soldiers. The soldiers began firing back, and in the confusion, the Lakota seemingly shot their woman and children.

There are a lot of problems with this narrative. First of all, if there indeed was a conspiracy in the camp to ambush the US Army, why weren't all of the weapons found in the first search? Secondly, it has been proven multiple times in past wars that the Sioux men were unwilling to do anything reckless to endanger their women and children. These, along with some other discrepancies, such as why the men in the camp would speak openly of their plans knowing that a translator was around, discredits Wells' account of the events entirely.

The most authentic version of the event surprisingly can be traced back to one of the US soldiers participating in the battle. Unlike many of his fellow soldiers, Private Hugh McGinnis of the 1st Battalion of the 7th Cavalry did not bear any goodwill toward the 7th Cavalry's actions on that day since he himself was gravely wounded by a shot from the Hotchkiss guns. McGinnis stayed silent about his side of the story for many years until a few months before his death. He wrote an extensive account of the events of his version of the story, which fits in with what the Lakota and the Native American rights activists had been trying to prove for years—that the Wounded Knee Massacre was not a battle but a mass genocide. His story was published posthumously in the January 1966 edition of the *Real West Magazine*.

According to McGinnis' account, when the US Army set up camp on the 28th, the four Hotchkiss guns accompanying the detachment were positioned on elevated ground near the entrance and the sides of the camp. Forsyth demanded that the Lakota give up their arms, which they were not very happy about, saying that without their hunting weapons, they would not be able to survive. Their answer seemed to greatly anger Forsyth, who ordered the soldiers to bring the men outside their tepees and then had every inch of the tents searched. Some of the Native American squaws (married women) started to protest about the random destruction of their property. At this point, the women and children were herded from their tents to the front of the camp while the men were ordered to go stand outside of the camp entrance.

McGinnis and about twenty other soldiers were stationed to guard the women when McGinnis heard a sudden gunshot. After that gunshot, the soldiers surrounding the encampment started firing on his position where the women and children were gathered. The first volley from the four Hotchkiss cannons was aimed at the civilians instead of the men in front of the entrance, killing or gravely injuring most of them outright, including the US soldiers guarding the Lakota encampment. McGinnis was wounded by one of the shrapnel-infused explosive Hotchkiss' rounds, which rained down death in a wide radius. From what he saw in his wounded state, men, women, and children within sight were all being slaughtered mercilessly as the Lakota men tried to fight back with clubs and other primitive weaponry.

What is so compelling about McGinnis' account is that he has no reason to lie on his deathbed and that it ties in with the theory that the 7th Cavalry fired on their own men, a fact that was constantly denied for a long time. Most importantly, it proves that General Miles' claims were not something conjured to hide his hand in the events of that day because, although he wasn't present during the massacre, he was the commanding officer of the forces in the area and had never meant for something like to this happen when he gave the order to arrest Sitting Bull.

The Lakota survivors also told their accounts of the events of that day, and they are incredibly similar to McGinnis' account. The one key difference in their version is that the US soldiers, while searching for weapons, were trying to estimate the age of the adult men in the camp. It seemed as if they were attempting to ascertain whether the men were old enough to have participated in the Battle of the Little Bighorn, a battle that still weighed heavy on the minds of those in the US military.

The tragic irony is that the events at Wounded Knee were the reverse of what occurred during the Battle of the Little Bighorn, which was a true battle that saw the decimation of the US Army instead of US civilians. At the Wounded Knee Massacre, there were only around 50 Lakota survivors. One survivor, a man named Dewey Beard, was crawling away from the scene of the massacre when he was found by five Oglala warriors who swiftly took him away. Dewey also managed to find his baby daughter, who was alive, but she sadly died the following year. He told his stories to his grandchildren, as the survivors were fairly old by the time their stories came to public light. So, the events of that terrible day have been painstakingly constructed by historians over the years from court records, as well as from diaries and journals that were left behind by many of the participants. Despite the lies told to justify the massacre as a battle after its occurrence, these documentations ultimately gave way to the truth.

One of the survivors, Alice Ghost Horse, later recounted the events leading up to that day to her grandchildren.

> By sundown we were completely surrounded by foot soldiers, all with rifles. My mother and I went down to the creek to pick up some wood and to go to the bathroom, but two soldiers followed us…so we hurried and came back with some sticks. At this time everyone went to bed we were all

tired out from this hard trip. Some of the young men were up all night to watch the soldiers. Some of the soldiers were drunk, saying bad things about the Lakota women.

Regarding the events of the day of the massacre, it seems highly probable that Yellow Bird's actions actually put the US soldiers on edge, not Black Coyote. According to Alice,

> A medicine man by the name of Yellow Bird…stood facing the east, right by the fire pit which was now covered up with fresh dirt. He was praying and crying. He was saying to the spotted eagles that he wanted to die instead of his people. He must sense that something was going to happen. He picked up some dirt from the fireplace and threw it up in the air and said, "This is the way I want to go back—to dust."

It is often agreed upon by modern historians that Philip Wells either instigated the massacre through mistranslation or was poor at the Lakota dialect, despite being half-Sioux. Alice's version of the events combined with the statements of Dewey Bear seems to indicate the former—Wells was simply instigating the US soldiers by mistranslating Yellow Bird's chants.

# Chapter 6- The Military Investigation of the Wounded Knee Massacre and the Medal of Honor Debacle

"If Forsyth was relieved because some squaws were killed, somebody had made a mistake, for squaws have been killed in every Indian war."

–General William T. Sherman

The above statement was made by the famous American war hero General Sherman upon hearing about the military trial of James Forsyth. That a man could dismiss the death of almost 120 women and children so casually might sound horrible today, but back in the last years of the American Indian Wars, this was the general sentiment in the US Army, including the secretary of war himself. It seems the only man who was upset over the massacre at Wounded Knee at that time was Major General Nelson Appleton Miles, who insisted on an official investigation of the event. General Miles was not aware that the men, instead of following the instructions he had given them, were massacring the Lakota. When he did learn of the massacre, he was extremely appalled. He also received a telegram that very day, praising the success of the army's efforts and the bravery of their men during the supposed battle.

After receiving praise from Washington for the military achievement at Wounded Knee, General Miles was definitely agitated, as expressed by his telegram to his superior the following day. On January 1st, 1891, General Miles sent the following telegram to Major General John Schofield, who was the commanding general of the US Army at the time:

> Your telegram of congratulations to the 7th Cavalry received, but as the action of the Colonel commanding will be a matter of serious consideration, and will undoubtedly be the subject of investigation, I thought it proper to advise you. In view of the above fact, do you wish your telegram transmitted as it was sent? It is stated that the disposition of four hundred soldiers and four pieces of artillery was fatally defective and large number of soldiers were killed and wounded by the fire from their own ranks and a very large number of women and children were killed in addition to the Indian men.

In reply, General Miles got the following telegram the next day:

> He [the president] hopes that the report of the killing of women and children in the affair at Wounded Knee is unfounded, and directs that you cause an immediate inquiry to be made and report the results to the Department. If there was any unsoldierly conduct, you will relieve the responsible officer, and so use the troops engaged there as to avoid its repetition.

Receiving the go-ahead, Miles went on to take actions to relive Forsyth of his command. But first, he needed substantial proof. For a primary evaluation of the event, Miles had already sent an investigation team under Captain F. A. Whitney the very evening he sent the telegram to Major General Schofield. The following night, he organized a team for burying the dead Native Americans, as they had to wait for a blizzard to break before doing so. Throughout the next two days, the team sent in by Miles conducted a battlefield investigation, piecing together the probable events by observing the battlefield. After three days of investigation, Whitney sent Miles the following letter:

> Sir: In compliance with instructions contained in your letter of January 1st, 1891, I have the honor to report that I have examined the ground where the fight with Big Foot's band occurred, [2] and counted the number of Indians killed and wounded, also number of ponies and horses with the following result: 82 bucks and 1 boy killed, 2 bucks badly wounded, 40 squaws killed, 1 squaw wounded, one blind squaw unhurt; 4 small children and 1 papoose killed, 40 bucks and 7 women killed in camp; 25 bucks, 10 women and 2 children in the canon [sic] near and on one side of the camp; the balance were found in the hills; 58 horses and ponies and 1 burro were found dead.

> There is evidence that a great number of bodies have been removed. Since the snow, wagon tracks were made near where it is supposed dead or wounded Indians had been lying. The camp and bodies of the Indians had been more or less plundered before my command arrived here. I prohibited anything being removed from the bodies of the Indians or the camp.

After forwarding these findings to Schofield, Miles received the following telegram, "I am directed by the Secretary of War to inform you that it was not the intention of the President to appoint a court of inquiry…You were expected yourself first to inquire into the facts and in the event of its being disclosed that there had been unsoldierly conduct, to relieve the responsible officer."

---

[2] Big Foot was the US military's nickname for Spotted Elk.

And this is where Miles made his biggest mistake—after receiving this telegram, he immediately relieved Forsyth of his command, which ultimately made most of the army personnel think that Miles had a personal agenda and needed someone to pin the massacre on. On January 5th, Miles concluded his investigation by sending the following telegram:

> The report of Colonel Forsyth and accompanying map shows what dispositions he made, and the map, presents one erasible [sic] fact, namely, the commands were so placed that the fire must have been destructive to some of their own men, while other portions of the troops were so placed as to be non-effective. It also appears that after a large number of their arms (47) had been taken away from the Indians, the fight occurred between the troops and Indians in close proximity. The additional map places the troops in somewhat different position. These positions were indicated by Major Whitside, 7th Cavalry as at [the] time [the] fight commenced. Captain Wallace was killed with a war club, others were stabbed with knives, and bows and arrows were used.
>
> The number of casualties were Captain Wallace and 24 men killed, Lieutenants Garlington, Gresham and Hawthorne and 33 men wounded. There were 82 Indian men killed and 64 women and children killed and buried on the ground, and four have since died of wounds, 30 Indians, including men, women and children, some wounded have reached the hostile camp on White Clay Creek, eight men, eleven women and sixteen children, all wounded and thirty women and children not wounded were brought to this place. Another body of Indians, numbering 63, 20 of whom were men, were captured on American Horse Creek, 25 miles from Wounded Knee by 15 scouts, and brought to this camp and disarmed without casualties occurring.

While the fight was in progress with Colonel Forsyth's command, about 150 Brule Indians left camp then en-route from the Bad Lands to this agency, and went down to the assistance or rescue of the Big Foot Indians. The troops had then become widely separated in chasing the Indians, and this band of Brules attacked Captain Jackson, and recaptured 26 prisoners.

Despite having nailed most of the facts correctly, Miles ultimately failed to prove them in the military tribunal, where many of the participants of the massacre gave sworn testimonies proving that Forsyth's character and actions were irreproachable. After a month-long investigation, Forsyth was released with all charges dropped. The result of this investigation was ultimately very damaging for General Miles. For trying to do the right thing, he was ostracized and looked down upon by his peers, something that he could not escape for the rest of his life. While Miles was doomed to obscurity, the Congress awarded twenty of the participants of the Wounded Knee Massacre Medals of Honor as well as recommendations to be promoted.

The Medals of Honor, the highest commendation one can receive in the US military, awarded to the men involved in the Wounded Knee Massacre have been highly debated for the last two decades and even longer in the Native American community. Many of the recipients were given medals based solely on the number of helpless Native Americans they slaughtered on that fateful day, some even pursuing those who were trying to hide from the slaughter. Although Medals of Honor were given more liberally during this time period, historians still believe that the number of medals awarded during this very one-sided "battle" is inconsistent when compared to other battles of the time period.

The atmosphere regarding Forsyth's trial was tense and a matter of national interest. Many argued that General Miles started to doggedly pursue Forsyth in order to keep his hands clean of the matter, as the Wounded Knee Massacre had been heavily published about in the papers. Despite crying for more Native American blood only two days before, many of the newspapers were already changing their tune after seeing the morbid and tragic photos of the dead Native Americans, and they were more than eager to label the event as a slaughter. This theory would be understandable if Miles actually needed a scapegoat to keep his hands clean in the public eye.

Another notable reason the investigation failed was that many of the investigators themselves were not supportive of Miles' decision to take Forsyth to trial. Major Samuel Whitside, one of the chief investigators, wrote the following in a letter to his wife: "The settlement of the Indian trouble has been a failure according to the plans arranged by Gen. Miles, and now someone must shoulder the responsibility and be sacrificed and from appearances Gen. F[orsyth] is the man selected, for other people to unload on."

And this was from within Miles' own camp. Other military officers had less favorable opinions. In a news article published in the *Evening Star* on January 5th, 1891:

> The relief of Col. Forsythe [sic] of his command of the seventh cavalry by Gen. Miles, which has been telegraphed east from unofficial sources, forms the prevailing topic of conversation around the War Department today. It is being talked about with a vigor and an openness of criticism that reminds old timers of the war times, when such troubles were frequent.
>
> One officer said to a Star reporter: "At this rate the Sioux troubles will grow to be just as bad as events of the first three years of the [Civil] war, when every officer with an independent command had not only an enemy in front of him but a court-martial behind him." Officers say that it was a grave error to order the relief of Col. Forsythe at this stage of the proceedings, and thus hold up a warning finger to every colonel in the little army around Pine Ridge, to tell them that

the death of each Sioux must be explained. It will have, it is openly asserted, a very demoralizing effect upon the enterprising bravery of the commanding officers in the field, and there are predictions that with the example that is being made of Col. Forsythe in full view there will hardly be a man in the army with any responsibility who will dare to do anything but take part in a negative campaign. The true inwardness of Gen. Miles' action in relieving Col. Forsythe has not yet come to light, but it is generally believed that this course was inspired by the officials here.

Neither Secretary Proctor nor Gen. Schofield are willing to say very much on the subject, although both practically admit that Gen. Miles did not act entirely upon his own responsibility. Secretary Proctor said to a Star reporter: "Gen. Miles did it. It is a very much mixed up matter and I may explain it later."

All these conflicting factors, as well as the fact that the president and secretary of war were supportive of the massacre, or as they termed it "a battle," trivialized the events, and it was ultimately covered up as an accident. While this is definitely not the first time this had happened, the blatant disregard of the truth and the ensuing cover-up brings some recent events to mind.

# Conclusion

The events during the Wounded Knee Massacre is truly an unspeakable tragedy and was just one of many that the Native Americans faced during the American Indian Wars. General Nelson Miles, who tried to clear things up by relieving the commanding general of the cavalry responsible for the event, ended up being unable to give any sort of satisfaction to the Lakota.

During the military trial against Forsyth, Forsyth stated that it was Miles who gave the written order to kill the Native Americans should negotiations fail and they get hostile. However, later on, when the orders were verified, it clearly stated that Forsyth was ordered to not even enter the camp, meaning that Forsyth was disobeying a direct order when he started searching the camp on December 29th, 1890. Many of the men accompanying him in the massacre backed up and justified his actions by lying that the Lakota attacked them first. Even nearly 130 years later, it is still a debated topic on whether the Wounded Knee Massacre was premeditated or due to the emotions of the US soldiers getting the better of them.

The Wounded Knee Massacre is one of the largest massacres to occur in the United States, and in 1990, the US Congress passed a resolution formally expressing their regret for the massacre. However, Wounded Knee hill, where the battle took place, is officially registered as the Wounded Knee Battlefield on the US National Register of Historic Places, and perhaps more importantly, the Medals of Honor the soldiers received while massacring the Lakota have still not been rescinded, although the process to rescind them began in June 2019 when the House of Representatives proposed a bill to remove the names of those men from the Medal of Honor roll.

We hope that this book has been successful in providing all the logical information and true historical facts of the Wounded Knee Massacre to establish what happened nearly 130 years ago. To stick to the established narrative that the massacre was an accident does a disservice to the innocent lives lost on that day, and we have tried our best to convey the true events to our readers by providing them with the best details and records we could access while researching for this book. Hopefully, this book will leave a solid impact on your mind and encourage you to study history in a more fact-based manner.

# Here's another book by Captivating History that you might be interested in

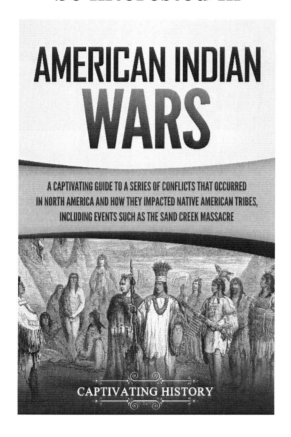

# THE BATTLE OF THE
# LITTLE BIGHORN

A CAPTIVATING GUIDE TO ONE OF THE MOST SIGNIFICANT ACTIONS
OF THE GREAT SIOUX WAR AND HOW CUSTER'S LAST STAND IMPACTED
THE NORTHERN CHEYENNE AND ARAPAHO TRIBES

CAPTIVATING HISTORY

# References

Brown, Dee, Bury My Heart at Wounded Knee (1971).

Jensen, Richard, et al., Eyewitness at Wounded Knee (1991).

Utley, Robert M., The Last Days of the Sioux Nation (1963).

Wells, Philip, "Ninety-six Years among the Indians of the Northwest," North Dakota History, 15, no. 2 (1948).

National Archives "Sioux Campaign, 1890-91," 635, 636, and 641.

Historical Society of Pennsylvania, Sioux Campaign 1890-91, vols. 1 and 2 (Philadelphia: Historical Society of Pennsylvania, 1919), 692.

Peter R. DeMontravel, The Career of Lieutenant General Nelson A. Miles from the Civil War through the Indian Wars, (1983).

James W. Forsyth, "Statement of Brigadier General James W. Forsyth, U.S. Army, concerning the investigations touching the fights with Sioux Indians, at Wounded Knee and Drexel Mission, near Pine Ridge, S. D., December 29 and 30, 1890," in Reports and Correspondence Related to the Army Investigations of the Battle at Wounded Knee and to the Sioux Campaign of 1890–1891, the National Archives Microfilm Publications (Washington: The National Archives and Records Service, General Services Administration, 1975), Roll 2, Target 4, Sep. 1, 1895 – Dec. 21, 1896, 7.

National Archives "Sioux Campaign, 1890-91," 785.

DeMontravel, Lieutenant General Nelson A. Miles, 359.

L. T. Butterfield, photo., "Big Foot. Dead," Deadwood Pictorial Works, Beinecke Rare Book & Manuscript Library, New Haven (http://brbl-dl.library.yale.edu/vufind/Record/3432007) accessed 27 Jul 2014.

Samuel L. Russell, "Selfless Service: The Cavalry Career of Brigadier General Samuel M. Whitside from 1858 to 1902," Master's Thesis, (Fort Leavenworth: U.S. Army Command and General Staff College, 2002), 144.

National Archives "Sioux Campaign, 1890-91," 824 (Whitney's report dated 3 Jan 1891).

L. T. Butterfield, "The Medicine Man taken at the Battle of Wounded Knee, S.D." (Chadron, Neb.: Northwestern Photographic Co., 1 Jan 1891), from Beinecke Rare Book & Manuscript Library, New Haven (http://brbl-dl.library.yale.edu/vufind/Record/3432008) accessed 27 Sep 2015; Carl Smith, Chicago Inter-Ocean, 7 Jan 1891, from Richard E. Jensen, R. Eli Paul, John E. Carter, Eyewitness at Wounded Knee (Lincoln, Neb.: University of Nebraska Press, 1991), 110.

Jacob F. Kent and Frank D. Baldwin, "Report of Investigation into the Battle at Wounded Knee Creek, South Dakota, Fought December 29th 1890," in Reports and Correspondence Related to the Army Investigations of the Battle at Wounded Knee and to the Sioux Campaign of 1890–1891, the National Archives Microfilm Publications (Washington: The National Archives and Records Service, General Services Administration, 1975), Roll 1, Target 3, Jan. 1891, 653-654. Hereafter abbreviated RIBWKC.

National Archives "Sioux Campaign, 1890-91," 828 (telegram from Schofield to Miles dated 6 January 1891).

Evening Star, "Relief of Col. Forsythe" (Washington, D. C., 5 Jan 1891).

DeMontravel, Lieutenant General Nelson A. Miles and the Wounded Knee Controversy.

George W. Cullum, Biographical Register of the Officers and Graduates of the U. S. Military Academy, vol. 2, (New York: James Miller, Publisher, 1879), 539-540, and 800-802.

Military Times, "Valor Awards for Frank Dwight Baldwin," Military Times Hall of Valor (https://valor.militarytimes.com/hero/907) accessed 27 Jul 2014; Robert H. Steinbach, "BALDWIN, FRANCIS LEONARD DWIGHT," Handbook of Texas Online.

(http://www.tshaonline.org/handbook/online/articles/fba43), accessed 27 Jul 2014, uploaded on 12 Jun 2010; Adjutant General's Office, "Baldwin, Frank D.," Letters Received, compiled 1871 – 1894, documenting the period 1850 – 1917, File Number: 3365 ACP 1875, image: 791 (http://www.fold3.com/image/1/303446614/) accessed 28 Jul 2014.

George E. Trager, photo., "Gen. Miles & staff during late Indian War at Pine Ridge Agcy," Northwest Photographic Co., Denver Public Library Digital Collection (http://cdm15330.contentdm.oclc.org/cdm/ref/collection/p15330coll 22/id/24030) accessed 27 Jul 2014.

Russell, "Selfless Service," 145; University of Washington, "James W. Forsyth Family Papers," (Seattle: University Libraries, 2011); Peter R. DeMontravel, A Hero to His Fighting Men: Nelson A. Miles, 1839-1925, (Kent: The Kent State University Press, 1998), 206.

National Archives "Sioux Campaign, 1890-91," 813-814 (letter from Miles to Schofield dated 5 Jan 1891).

https://blog.oup.com/2015/12/wounded-knee-nelson-a-miles-lakota-justice/.

Made in United States
North Haven, CT
23 September 2023

41898516R00036